# Risk

# Risk

Poems by

Marydale Stewart

Kelsay Books

© 2017 Marydale Stewart. All rights reserved. This material may not be reproduced in any form, published, reprinted, recorded, performed, broadcast, rewritten or redistributed without the explicit permission of Marydale Stewart. All such actions are strictly prohibited by law.

ISBN:13- 978-1-947465-17-6

*Kelsay Books*
Aldrich Press
www.kelsaybooks.com

To my friend
Barry Brukoff
who remembers
what I remember

# Acknowledgments

Grateful acknowledgement is made to the editors and publishers of the following publications and one radio program in which these poems first appeared:

*After Hours:* "On Walden" and "High Plains Revenant"
*DoveTales, An International Journal of the Arts, "Refugees and the Displaced" a publication of Writing for Peace:* "Blue Snow," "Peace on Mars," and "Standing Rock 2016"
*Fredericksburg Literary Review:* "The Walking Man" and "Ag Museum"
*Friends Journal:* "Silence"
*Secrets and Dreams Anthology* (Kind of a Hurricane Press) "Risk"
*The Aurorean:* "The Gaze"
*Writers Resist:* "Standing Rock 2016,"
*WNIJ* (NPR affiliate, Rockford and DeKalb, IL): "The Daily News"

# Contents

| | |
|---|---|
| After Moving | 11 |
| Putting By | 12 |
| Winter Morning, 1944 | 14 |
| That's Who I Was | 15 |
| Autobiography | 16 |
| The Daily News: A Pantoum | 17 |
| Machines | 18 |
| Inventory | 19 |
| To My Cardiologist | 20 |
| On Walden | 21 |
| The Walking Man | 22 |
| Not This Time | 23 |
| Standing Rock, 2016 | 25 |
| What the World Needs | 26 |
| The Passion | 27 |
| Meeting, Illinois | 29 |
| Silence | 30 |
| Echo | 31 |
| Blue Snow | 33 |
| Risk | 34 |
| Murder Scene | 35 |
| February 28 in Illinois | 37 |
| Opening Out | 38 |
| High Plains Revenant | 39 |
| Tomorrow | 42 |
| The Gaze | 43 |
| Dick Whittington's Luck | 44 |
| Maud in the Poet's House | 48 |
| Rescue Work | 49 |
| That'll do, Zelda | 50 |
| Five Ways of Looking at a Starling | 51 |
| Wrensong | 53 |

| | |
|---|---:|
| Marsh Hawk | 54 |
| Spirit Horse | 55 |
| Deer Dancing | 56 |
| Wasp Nest | 57 |
| Tornado Warning | 58 |
| Ag Museum | 59 |
| The Humane Way | 61 |
| Peace on Mars | 62 |
| The Decision | 63 |
| The Reader's Song | 64 |
| Reader, I Married Him, but… | 66 |
| Timor Mortis: In Praise of the Makars | 67 |
| Letting Go | 68 |

About the Author

# After Moving

I sift through boxes left unpacked
from several moves ago:
my mother's Browning, a faded hat,
old photographs of straight-haired,
sepia-stained women grouped
solemnly before an unknown hand.

If I traveled back in time,
I'd hear again the silver stillness
of my old home, hear again
November rain break its slant
against a wavy window pane,
see again a rush of moon-knit
maple branches in a raveling wind
while I wait for the blue light of morning
to shine on familiar sights.

If I traveled back in time,
would that gleaming road from here to the past
lose its allure, grow dim, and disappear?
Those shifting, glinting shards
of memory, those moments that rise
flashing in my heart like bits of broken
mirrors: wouldn't they dissolve
and lie unperceived
in all those ordinary days?

# Putting By

One morning long ago
just after the war ended
a produce truck overturned
on a narrow paved road
and was abandoned.

Most of the fruit was bruised,
no good to anyone but the women
in a nearby crossroads town,
six unnamed streets set down
in cornfields that reached out
to the feet of shimmering horizons.

The women heard the news
on the four-party phone lines,
arrived with baskets, pails, sacks,
anything they could use
to carry home the fruit to can.

My great-aunt, my grandmother,
and all their neighbors
canned all day and into the night
through the corn-creaking, locust-wailing,
unforgiving Illinois summer heat,
using and sharing their sugar supply,
disagreements and gossip forgotten,
children enlisted and sent on errands,
small soldiers on a new front.

Kettles and cookers burped and steamed,
row after row of dripping gleaming jars
on shelves and tabletops

pinged their lids, cooling, sealing.
Even with sugar still scarce,
they canned all day and into the night.

Row after row in basements, cupboards,
summer kitchens, through cooling weather
they waited, like medals for valor,
for winter dinner parades.

# Winter Morning, 1944

Under one featherbed
and on top of another,
I'd move a toe
then pull it back
to its night-warmed hole.

I'd listen half awake
to muffled kitchen sounds
downstairs,
mother and grandmother
querying, planning,
talking of rationing, someone's furlough,
what's left of summer canning,
the harsh winter over there,
kept to a murmur
what seven-year-olds need not know.

Downstairs in a rush,
I'd find my clothes
spread out to warm
on an open oven door,

shrug in a hurry
into slacks, sweater,
find fresh mixed oleo
ready to spread on toast:
unaware that this place
in the silent center
of farm fields
was at that moment
the safest I'd ever know.

## That's Who I Was

I noticed today, couldn't help it,
how the light touch of a friend's hand
on my elbow made my steps more steady
down the broad meetinghouse stairway.

Now mind you, it wasn't long ago
that I could stack a load of hay—a ton or more—
and keep my footing on the slippery loft floor,
chat up the folks on the rack below, make a couple of nests
for barn cats by stacking the bales just so,
admire the dimpled spines of my horses from up above,
plan what I'd make for supper, then go home
and mow the yard.

That's who I was.

Yes, that girl, that woman, that busy sprinter
through three-fourths of a century: I still see
her picture in my albums, looking ready for anything.
But just between us, she didn't know half what I know now.

I wish I could have told her
to slow down and listen:
love what you've got, do no harm,
don't throw anything away,
but when you have to,
throw it all away.

# Autobiography

From the year I was five
until I was almost ten
I was a horse, a different horse
from day to day
or for weeks on end.

Whatever horse I was,
untamed black, docile paint,
heroic gleaming bay,
I knew how to shake my mane,
whinny piercingly, and snort and paw
the ground, often at the dinner table
or when meeting family friends.

Then at last my imagined horse
found its living counterpart
and then another and another.
But when the last one died,
I was suddenly alone, too wise
and conscious of decorum
to whinny piercingly, paw the ground,
or shake my gray old mane.

# The Daily News: A Pantoum

Today it will be cloudy, with a thunderstorm or two.
A war may end; leaders have agreed to meet.
Global warming evidence is presented for review.
A homer gets the Cubs a second winning streak.

Many wars could end if leaders would agree to meet.
I wonder what you'd think if you were here
about the Cubs or anybody's winning streak,
about the wars, elections, or if the weather will be clear.

I wonder what you'd think if you were here—
but the world has changed since we were first together.
There's more war, new elections, a new variety of fear.
We thought we'd be the way we were forever.

But we'll never be the way we were when we were first together;
our daily news is archived now.
We thought we'd be the way we were forever
while the hills turn green in spring and the fates allow.

Our daily news is archived now.
Sea levels rise, cities drown in hurricanes.
Though the hills are greening now, the fates did not allow
that we should ever meet again.

Sea levels rise, cities drown in hurricanes;
global warming evidence is presented for review.
I dreamed that we had met on a green and windy hill again
and it was cloudy with a thunderstorm or two.

# Machines

In the winter they told me
my heart's not efficient anymore,
not working hard enough.
They explained the many ways
my heart might fail to perform.

I thought about this quite a lot,
listening, cautious, apprehensive
during those dull abbreviated days
that are over in the middle
of the afternoon, over before
the day's work is done.

In the spring, it was different.
My mower was returned,
new O rings, carburetor cleaned,
blades sharpened—engine roaring
with hoarse authority.  Right away,
I made several fine green lanes
across my lawn, no more stuttering,
clogging, malingering. Sparrows, grackles,
starlings dived into the heaped-up fragrant wake
for their dinners, robins stalked behind.

Like them, I'd caught the irresistible,
snapped it up, was the better for it.

# Inventory

In my garage, tools lean against the wall.
Several kinds of pitchforks, one made to clean
a shavings-bedded horse stall.
No use here in town.
Shovels, yes–
an ordinary snow shovel. A deep scoop shovel
I'd used to fill a wheelbarrow,
even a trenching spade.

In a bucket, farrier's tools:
nippers to trim a hoof,
the big two-sided rasp
I'd learned to hold by both ends,
drawing one way only
across the unshod hoof
the horse had let me place
between my knees.
Hoof knives gone, lent years ago to friends.

In the house, a claw hammer and a ball-peen.
Phillips and straight screwdrivers.
Some allen wrenches.
Best of all, a crowbar. Not enough pliers.
What happened to the Channellocks
I'd once used in a well pit
to shut off water to a broken pipe?

In my seventh decade now,
tools are for indoors:
a knitting needle for slow drains,
a delete key for composing poetry,
a straightened paper clip for everything,
and that good old crowbar
to replace finesse.

# To My Cardiologist

So, you ask
to see inside my heart,
see if its slippery, perfect parts
are still doing what they were programmed
to do millions of years ago,
propelling that complex brew
called blood in and out of all
its corridors, doors, gates, hallways.
and rooms, as it ran through the lives
of mastodons and shrews.

O most esteemed physician,
having spent more hours
reading EKGs than poems,
you may not be aware
that when our language was only
in its adolescent years, sounding out
the songs of mythic life,
heart and courage meant the same.

You could ask instead
what my heart's intentions are,
does it aim to march to a cause,
step to its own enduring beat,
scour guns from the streets,
welcome immigrant children,
socialize medicine once and for all,
protect pit bull dogs,
play Bach in grocery stores,
prohibit children's football,
serve the helpless,
and study war no more?

# On Walden

On this ordinary beach
(if you pretend it's just a beach where people come to play),
I walked the narrow reach to the water
and stood for a moment, not wanting to wade.

At the pond's edge I knelt, holding out my chalice
to the water folding and unfolding at my feet.
The chalice (a small glass bottle) filled
slowly, then at last grew heavier in my hand.
This chalice I then took from Concord
back across the land.

Someday, when I can't be there to explain
why that chalice came
back across the land
back to its quiet reign in my kitchen cupboard,
someone will hold it up, wonder at it,
and pour it down the drain.

# The Walking Man

There he is, on the shoulder
of the two-lane road
out of town. Warm overcast day
just after 9 in the morning.
A resolute walk, not rapid
but strong. Backpack.
I pass him, then drive on.

Rearview mirror shows a few seconds
of short white beard, lean face.
Jeans flap against long shins.
Nothing ahead for him but a long walk
to the next town past new-planted corn.
Now light rain dots my windshield.
I should stop.

But I'm a woman alone.
I drive on. A dip in the road and he's gone.

Later on, my business done,
I'm halfway home on the same road.
It's almost noon. There he is,
the same walk, and there's the backpack.
I should stop, turn around.
Wouldn't take long, just back to town.

But the rain's ended.
Lunch is waiting. I drive on.

Since then,
every time I drive that road again
I look for him, to make amends.

# Not This Time

*for Barack Obama, Fall 2008*


We the people—
we who tend our aging parents'
daily chores, drop our time cards
in the slot,
set down our mops,
reach for the bill at a working lunch,
shop at stores for children's shoes,
wake up from surgery,
count our tips,
correct our son's or daughter's batting stance,
pick up dog poop,
collect mid-term exams,
borrow to pay bills past due—
we vote for presidents, too,
and we'd like to know
who to choose
to fight the wounded
dragon and help the country
meet its own invented destiny.
We're waiting for a scandal or
a slip of rhetoric
to tip the scale. Four years ago,
we despised one candidate
and praised the other,
and we'll do it again
over and over
till we forget forever who we were.

But not this time.
There's one among us
who speaks as if he'd

lift the fog from the city on the hill,
and bring in a new America,
people with passion,
people who tell the truth
and live it,
people who'd dare
to say yes
to being decent to one another.

This time, I feel us together
spinning backward, to the days when
truths were re-born in the New World
and history began again for us.
This time, we know already
that he's the one
and it stops us in our tracks
and takes our breath away—
Carl Sandberg and Vachel Lindsay
would have sung of him—
this time, it's a slender rough voiced man
whose emblematic roots
combine the place where
humankind began with
our own heartland's history
and I watch almost
with agony to see
if he'll succumb
to needs of strategy
and shady strike-and-scuffle deals
and let opponents dent
his clean, sheer courage—
Please, not this time.

# Standing Rock, 2016

I sent my heart, that figurative muscle,
that metaphor, that emblem,
to go in my stead to Standing Rock

where my feet have never known the steady earth,
that certain sky, the remembered places the wind has been,
where I've never known another living being as my own,
where the people came together
building, feeding, singing, hoping,
where grief and hope called them all together,
where they're showing a nation how to be a nation.

I've been to other places where the land I stood on
spoke to me with a blackbird's call, a silvered silent creek,
where I sheltered in the humming wind for days, nights,
and the long singing years.

Helpless I am in love and grief,
for the earth is my home, wherever I am.

# What the World Needs

Asked to give a presentation
and lead a discussion,
I chose The Light of the World,
and told how Holman Hunt
painted it outdoors at night
by lantern light, bundled
against London's November cold
a century and a half ago,
how he and the Pre-Raphaelite
Brotherhood tried to save their world
with purity, truth, and integrity,
how he painted a last copy of it
when he was nearly blind,
how it toured the Empire
for eight million viewers,
how it came home
to St. Paul's, and how Londoners
a generation and a half later
risked their lives
to save it and the cathedral
from the fires of the Blitz with
sandbags and stirrup pumps.

When I was done, a man said:
The world needs another painting.

# The Passion

In a curved plastic chair
at the foot of a paper-sheeted couch,
I wait for my flu shot.

Centered in a pale green wall
is a silver crucifix, gleaming
under a cubed fluorescent ceiling light.
His left knee is raised a little above the right leg.
His chest is arched. Both surfaces sparkle
under the light. His head is tilted, chin down.

I begin to wonder, as I sit in the quiet,
how the people nearby can be so calm.
The figure is tiny, but his agony is monstrous.

It reaches out into the room, under the door,
up the hallway, around and behind
the appointment desk, out to the parking lot.
And still no one notices.

He can speak only in short gasps
because his chest has filled with fluid.
They drove the nails
through his wrists to bear his weight.
Palms rip apart too easily.
He can exhale only by bearing down on his nailed feet
and then stretching up.

All over his body, his muscles cramp and do not let go.
He is in shock from blood lost when they flayed his back
all the way to the bone. He has been butchered alive.

He will die at last because he cannot breathe.
To be sure they get the matter finished
before the sun goes down,
they'll spear him through his side, a short thrust
for the long Roman shaft.

But I think it is still daylight now,
although there are no windows here.
In the hallway, there is conversation.
A nurse enters, asks which arm I'll offer for injection.

## Meeting, Illinois

I sidle through, knowing the wide door creaks,
join others seated in the narrow cushioned pew.
No one stirs, all having settled in,
as Quakers say. Deep slow breaths now;
I give myself to silence.

Fragmented, I resist thought—
an annoying friend (peace, just peace),
an errand (it'll wait). And so do we,
silent, together, patient, while through
the windows under the wide high ceiling
a song sparrow's three-note trill
enters from the trees outside. It resounds
against the white wainscoted walls
that have surrounded Friends
in Meetings here for a century and a half.

On this land they planned
the routes of freedom seekers from the South,
prayed to end the Civil War, held no man
or woman higher than another.
In my old age, I came back here
to sit with them, encircled, drawn in,
a listener once again.

# Silence

Odd that I'd remember flying alone
under a summer ceiling of benign cumulus
as a silent time. There was always
the snarl of the old Lycoming
that made talk impossible, even if there'd been
someone else along.

Below, a stitched and measured Midwest world
tilted when I banked, fell away
in a climb. I was a kitten on a rug, pouncing
on the elements in my J3 Cub, wings and rudder
like flung-out thoughts of lift and motion.

Often I'd dip a wingtip through a cloud,
not a big one—too well trained for that—
but bigger than a wisp, just to see
what it looked like sliced in half.

And I had moments
in this silent towering sky
when I simply looked around,
suddenly abashed
as if I'd wandered into
a wealthy neighbor's private realm.

# Echo

A place where railroad tracks once
lay cold on harsh gravel
became a grassy path a long time ago
bordered by trees
hiding the path from the narrow waves
of stubble-ribbed fields
on either side. There I am again.
And there I watch my soul
step away from me.

She walks to the entrance
of this long green-leafed
tunnel, where mock orange, honeysuckle,
and bird cherry lean and arch across
the dim cool path.
I watch her with envy.
She does not want to turn back.
She is not waiting for anything.
She does not know haste.

She stands still now.
She does not seem to see the beloved faces
who graced my past life
emerging from the green darkness ahead,
one in front of another. I watch with hope.

I watch but cannot move toward them.
She will not let them see me.
She has no longing for the past.
I watch with disbelief, then anger.
How can she do this to me?

I wake to hear an echo of her
voice: You need to grow.
You are not ready.
not ready, not ready.

# Blue Snow

From morning through mid-day
it snowed, wrinkling the air,
throwing tree-tops at the sky.

Guarded by windows, furnace,
I heard the snow hiss
and thump the corners
of my house.

It's over at dusk.
The snow turns blue,
blue on rooftops, porches,
a complacent imperious blue.

I admire it
but as I watch, it becomes

the blue and silent child
I've just seen pictured
in the news

whose family across the world
fled explosions of blood.
Under another snow,
he died hungry and cold.

# Risk

In mid-winter, the cold
licks at my windows
like a scavenging wolf
and stuns me into stillness.
I wait for rescue.

Once there were stories to warn us.
Persephone wandered to danger
in a garden blooming under an avuncular sun.
Eurydice's return to daylight
was foiled by her lover's desperate glance.
Europa playfully twined flowering vines
on the horns of a white bull calf.

Even so, I dream myself released.
I plant sunflowers along the fence.
I plant marigolds, dahlias, and asters,
zinnias, impatiens, alyssum, dianthus.
Trusting the sun, I dismiss
our perilous histories.

# Murder Scene

In the middle of my back yard,
atop a fresh fall of snow,
lies a murder scene.
An explosion of feathers
scatters like arrows pointing
to a shallow hole in roiled snow.
On one side of the hole
is a hieroglyph: fanned
fingerlike lines trace an event
that must have led to death.

Let's review the evidence.
Ladies and gentlemen of the jury,
I ask you to imagine this:
A hawk sat still and alone
on the fence of this very yard
earlier today.

She spotted a small bird
by itself a short distance away.
Its companions darted
and fussed at the bird feeder.
She rose from the fence
with a startling revelation
of her great wings, then achieved
a marvelous thing, arced
her body, claws extended far ahead,
and landed grasping this small bird.
As she landed, her wings
trailed wide in the snow,
leaving those fanlike marks.
Then she rose with her prey

in a shower of small gray
and brown feathers.

The prosecution rests.
There is no defense.
And the jury, in spite of
circumstantial evidence,
cannot find the accused
guilty of a crime.

# February 28 in Illinois

This joked-about changeable weather
has stayed the same too long.
Last week a flock of robins
stopped all day in a neighbor's yard,
pretending sub-zero temperature
wasn't a problem for them.
Next day, though, they were gone.

Teenagers look at the calendar, abandon
winter coats, then walk stiffly around outdoors
with hoodies wrapped close. I teeter on my icy path
to feed stray cats behind my garage.

Something's gone wrong, I know. In July,
we'll find our lawnmowers
won't work in foot-deep snow.

# Opening Out

*Glade Park, Colorado*


Rusty lies the mesa in September sun.
Sometimes we'd go there
for respite from ourselves.
Deep in aspen groves
we'd go, winding upward,
our old jeep grinding through
the grace and silence,
through stands of dappled aspen.

Once we topped a rise and stopped,
surprised. Below us, in flattened pastoral,
lay a nameless lake, a passive host
to some half-dozen men and women.
They sat and stood, fishing, in groups of two or three,
reposeful but intent. For a moment they blended
with the lake, their chairs, the scattered trees,
and shimmered there, frozen into memory.

# High Plains Revenant

*west of Fort Larned, Kansas*

1995

I step slowly from the small gray car.
Here, the Santa Fe trail is wide, not a pair
of grassy ruts a wagon's width apart.
To remember the travelers
you have to look away
and all at once you see
in the distance a wide depression
in the leaning, headed grass. Then
without warning, like a storm, it blows
into your mind: the shouts, the snorting
of the horses and mules,
the rattle, billow, and creak of the wagons.

Eager for sensation, re-creation,
I sink into the grass, reach for a handful
of stems to grasp—
sharp-edged and alive—
alive as I was then.

1869

I tried to move with the sway,
with the wagon's jolt and strain,
but they took me off the wagon
when the bleeding began again.

They laid me on the grass—
that fine, soft tan-with-autumn
grass, and the sky tilted above.

Oh my husband, oh my love,
had you but waited another month
before you lay with me at last
in your mother's fine sleigh bed,
I might have gone all the way
to the town of Santa Fe.

Now too soon, too soon,
came the probing, dragging pain.
I heard my screams from far away
as the prairie hummed around my head
and murmured in buzzing flowers.
The meadowlarks' bell-like song
tolled out all the long hours.
And then all at once I was done.

Have they taken you, my babe,
all alone from that cobalt blue
and golden place, with the blood-soaked
fine tan grass? Have they taken you
on to Santa Fe?

1995

The voices fade, the earth is still;
only a pillar of yellow dust
hovers over the trail. The grass is crushed
where I lie. I turn my head to find
my car, but there is only
a small rounded stone.
The grass is soaked with blood
once more, again my own.

All the wagons are gone;
I am the only one
left behind.

# Tomorrow

Her voice, blurred by age
and dental attrition,
is charged with certainty.
Tomorrow, she tells me,
she's going home.

Her stroke has reduced her life
to essentials: meals, Bingo,
basketball on the nursing home TV,
trying to walk in physical therapy,
and her need for her cat.

I've been caring for her cat.
He sits purring near me,
wanting only extra treats
and someone's attention.

She knows nothing of this feline perfidy.
Every day, she tells everyone
she's going home tomorrow.
But she has lost her apartment,
her few possessions, and her mobility.

I'll find someplace, she says.
I'll sleep on the floor.
I don't need furniture.
Just my cat. I just want my boy.

# The Gaze

I'd compare
the black-eyed drill of this gaze
to any I can remember
from any lover I can recall.
The owner of the gaze
is yesterday's stray:
a cat with clumped black fur
and prominent spine, resigned to waiting.

Yesterday, swept inside, he ate with intensity,
allowed injection of sterile fluids under his skin
and other miracles to occur.
Today he sits on a rumpled window-seat cover
in window sun, ignoring windowed birds outside,
to look at me while I lean over him.

I'm no Iseult to his Tristan
but in this moment,
grounded in this instant,
this gaze makes my history.

# Dick Whittington's Luck

*at the Whittington Stone, London*

Today he looks over his shoulder,
this stone cat, as if forever watching
for some Falstaffian fool to snatch him again,
toss him in a box with a lot of
evil smelling rags and clanking metal
tools, to land on a ship
bound for Africa.

He may be watching, too, for his friend—
the bony boy he walked behind
down into London Town
a decade or two before the century turned
to fourteen hundred. Once there,
they slept in a rough hut hollowed
out of firewood. The boy worked
days and nights in a black and smoking kitchen
while its great house blazed with light
and guests came and left in a proud
entourage on robber-ridden roads.

The real cat hid, hungry,
feet tucked under matted tabby fur,
when the boy was beaten, then
took the treats of bread, rarely meat,
the boy saved for him,
and waited for the sobbing to end.

He could not know that he would
be ship's cargo soon—one of many
motley gifts wrested from
the hands and hearts of servants

in the great houses.
A bitter honor, this, and the boy
could only crouch, avoiding once again
the descending fist, the hoarse shout.

And so it happened—the lurching
brutal box, the slippery deck!
In time, the cat learned to catch
the foul huge rats
by leaping across their backs, twisting down
to a fatal grip on the neck. And in time

the men's callused feet avoided him; almost
deferentially, roughened hands tossed
scraps his way. Of the black water beyond
he lived in terror.

Nor could he know his fame would spread
ashore, when the ship docked under
the white Moroccan sun with a shudder
and grind of wood, lethal coils of hempen
lines flying into the pungent, sweaty air.
Shouts of the men and bone-shattering
crashes of cargo, barreled and boxed,
tore at his senses and nerves until
he found the safest lair the little ship
afforded: the master's bunk.

The sailors found the cat and dragged him out.
We know only this: He would work at what he did
better than any cat had ever done
in this strange ancient land:

stalking, pouncing, routing
the teeming squealing hordes of mice and rats
year after year, to the delight
of all of Barbary. They say he sat
on rich pillows after that, lapping
creamy camel milk until his tabby coat
turned to silk, his sunken sides
expanded comfortably.

But the boy! Without the cat,
his world grew darker, each moment
congealed in pain and loss.
Despairing at last,
he slipped out in the night, climbing
to Highgate where, weak and chilled,
he sat to rest, head in hands.

Then from nearby St. Mary's, the bells
spoke out, voices in the dark, that said to him:
"Turn again, turn around—
thrice Lord Mayor of London Town!"
They found him there, staring down
at old London Town, where hope rose
once again in the form of three
bejeweled citizens, bearing a sack of gold.

"Your fortune, sir," they said to him.
"The Sultan of Morocco claims your cat
to be his own, says he's worth his weight
in gold for every year he lives.
And he'll make sure he lives
in princely splendor with never
a feline care in the world."

If London streets were ever paved
in gold, they gleamed then
in that green and misty dawn—
for with his sea-borne riches,
Dick Whittington did indeed become
thrice Lord Mayor of London Town.

And forever after, every tabby cat
that sees earth's light has borne
a special mark: a W or an M, whichever
you prefer, between its ears in silken fur.

# Maud in the Poet's House

Along comes Maud:
a silver tabby half-grown.
Elusive, joyful, sudden,
owner of my bed pillow,
licker of ice cream bowls.

I know she lives another life
in another place hidden to me,
like a poem growing.
No slow stretch of greeting there—
instead the low baneful stalk:
she's all claws and ripping teeth, blood
and tiny entrails, desperate squeal.
She does murder in all degrees
in her primordial other-land.

# Rescue Work

Cat and kittens doing fine,
but little mother bit me pretty hard:
this from a colleague in rescue work.
Five discarded lives, four of them new,
are assured safe harbor now
and we know her hand will heal.

Later, we'll do the right thing,
send this gallant creature into surgery,
skillfully violated and treated for post op pain.
I know we have to do this but oh—
how I hate our domination—
they're not perfect anymore
when we're done with saving them.

# That'll do, Zelda

She sets her feet
in the doorway
as if she can't remember
where she was going or why.
Or maybe in her mind she's running
flat-out down the long straight
Kansas road we lived on.
Or herding the ducks
that came with the place
when we bought it.
Or fixing a barn cat
with her border collie stare.

She hasn't done much
in the way of real work,
like some of her kind. After the third time
she'd come the mile or so
from the neighbors,
I said, "Well, I'm keeping her now."
It was OK with them; they said
they didn't care
one way or the other.

Now, fifteen years later
and five hundred miles back east,
we're both afraid we might
fall on the stairs. Who'll go first,
I wonder. Either way, whatever
will she do without me?

# Five Ways of Looking at a Starling

I.
While I weed my flower bed, I hear
domestic hustle behind and above me.
In a crevice under my eaves,
unmended for years,
starlings whirr and stir.

II.
I think of Shakespeare
whose fault it was the birds
are here, saying not "Mortimer"
but whatever else they might hear
and mindlessly repeat.

III.
In my street
and from east coast to west,
they've become indeed
*sturnus vulgaris*,
knowing not and caring less
that capricious humanity
has lost interest in the idea
of birds mentioned by The Bard.

IV.
In my yard,
dark bodies line a power wire
like fists, shoving each other,
clacking, gurgling, whistling,
flapping scolds.

V.
But behold!
In a sudden slant of sun
they glow in blue, purple, green,
shining imperial white dots,
wing feathers
folded up in perfect rows.

# Wrensong

This summer, before and after rain,
somewhere in the maples
or in the past-bloom lilacs
in my yard,
a wren's arpeggio rang out
over and over again.

Sometimes I spent hours
in my car
stopping at drive-up windows,
getting out and back in,
parking in concrete lots,
pausing at automatic doors,
enduring the din
of commercial chores.

While I was gone,
the wren kept on singing
in my yard.
His song caroled me home
over and over again.

Today my yard is still.
Late summer locusts tell
of heat and tired grass,
and I think the wren has left.

He must be visiting somewhere; he'll return.
He's here, I know it. He can't resist;
in a moment, surely, he'll sing again.

# Marsh Hawk

You of long wings, quick
tumbling into wind, are like
all things of common joy—
quiet squares of sunlit windows,
patterned wash of clouds
on buckskin fields.

Your sweep of exaltation,
your steep chandelles
mock lesser hunters.
My life, too, seeks
its own elusive prey:
stopped diapason,
song sparrow's triad,
someone's voice around a corner—
all things of sudden joy.

# Spirit Horse

I saw what happened to you.
You were never safe from them—
rider, owner, groom—
under saddle,
at rest in your stall,
being led to pasture,
never safe from the undeserved blow
across your front legs, on your face,
the stripe of the whip along your flank.
You were never safe
no matter where you were.

I know why you whirled
when they came after you,
why you flattened your ears in fear,
why you lunged, teeth bared,
at everyone who came near you.

I know what happened to you.
You were given the good death
after your owners abused you.

Where are you now, Spirit Horse?
Have you forgotten your tormentors,
dropped your fine head to graze
in an Elysian pasture?

If I were there with you
I would see myself reflected
deep in your purple-eyed gaze,
a penitent from the human race.

# Deer Dancing

On a windless autumn night
I drove along a narrow road
through scrub woods.
On one side black-rimmed by trees
a fallow field opened underneath the moon.
There six or seven deer
danced in the light.

I saw one deer leap high
above the ground
in a version of capriole;
another reared and rode
the black and silver air.

The hunters all had gone away,
wind-borne cry of danger silenced.
From the dusk-knit trees
the deer came out to play
in the free and quiet
whiteness of the night.

# Wasp Nest

At first I thought it was just a loner
drifting away from my shadow,
not that it needed to fear me,
then later I saw more of them glide
into and around a small cavity
in a patch of wet ground.

I spoke to them in my mind:
It seems you like the water that drips
here. I'll just turn on this tap,
pull out the hose and water the grass.
Then I'll be out of your way.

Or, I could soak a rag with gasoline
and drop it over your hole,
or put a window screen over your nest
to hold you down
while I spray you to kingdom come.
I could use this hose you like so well
to drown you in your own home.

Instead, let's just
leave each other alone.

# Tornado Warning

Thunder had a darker voice today,
deeper, invincible, stern.

Not stalking
like a bully
but in a cops-and-robbers
stake-out
sitting there,
rattling electrons
or whatever makes the thunder
speak of overheated insults.

Here's the siren, now.
Electric keening like a dagger
slides between the folds
of gray and yellow air.

It's meant to tell us:
If you're outside,
take cover, get inside somewhere.

Instead, we leave our houses,
go outdoors,
stand around
in flickering dusk
so we can better fear
the rolling thump and shudder
that's out there in the air approaching town.

# Ag Museum

It was the pork chop barbecue
that tipped the scale for me. Otherwise
I'd have stayed home—too hot and dry
to be outside this August Sunday.
We went in three cars, rendezvoused
in the white dust of the gravel
behind the pre-fab metal building.
Plenty of people there, too,
ranged along the picnic tables
shaded under canvas, breeze-cooled.

One by one we finished lunch: chop in a bun,
mound of potato salad, helping of sweet brown
baked beans, best I'd had in a long time.
In the cavernous museum, a perspiring man
in a nineteenth century shirt, vest, and frock coat
told us he was John Deere, told us how
he'd made the first steel moldboard plow
and how he kept the business going
through its Grand Detour days and then
for the generations in Illinois and finally the world.
We all knew the story but it was good to hear it again,
a pleasant reminder of where we'd been.

After that, I walked around, inspected history
arranged, dusted, described on white cards
alongside mannequins resting after hard lives.
In alcoves were quilts, furnishings, stone crocks and churns.
Then the tools: walking plows, a grain drill, a corn sheller.
Then tractors: a brilliant green John Deere,
a restored Fordson, a rusted but dignified Oliver.

Last, in a room apart were the uniforms and guns,
the other side of this kind and hopeful past.
Faded tunics, belts, caps, insignia of command and courage,
sat stiffly upright on mute forms, shadowed and still.

From the quiet core of life, from the center
of these farmlands, from the cradle of the land itself,
the young men went to war. With new sets of tools
and new seasons to understand, they learned to kill.

# The Humane Way

In a radio interview, a Utah lawmaker
said his state has a real problem.
We can't get the lethal drugs we need
to perform executions, he said.
Those European companies
just won't sell them to us.

The legislature has proposed a solution,
however: execution by firing squad.
It's more humane than lethal injection,
anyway. The individual, he said, dies quicker.

As for that time in 1879
when they missed and it took
27 minutes for the man to die, well,
we do it differently now, he said.
With restraints, the individual
can't flinch or twist away.

Members of the firing squad are volunteers,
he said. So staffing's no problem.
There's always an abundance of officers
who want to be on the firing squad.

# Peace on Mars

Go to Mars, young humankind,
live in manufactured atmosphere
walled up in caves and tunnels safe
from red dust storms and radiation.
Live among strangers with whom you'll die
before your time.

Before you leave, they'll edit your genes
so you can live on less oxygen.
You'll become frail in breath, bone,
and muscle mass, never again able
to live on Earth.

After the jubilation and farewells,
after the terror of departure,
set yourselves the only challenge left
and find the answer in your past:

Never, never cry havoc—
and forever, oh, forever
hold hard the dogs of war.

# The Decision

With respect for the love and energy
your creator invested in you,
I hesitate a moment—
yes, resisting guilt—
and stay my hand, so to speak,
before I do this.

I know when I do,
all further movement will cease.
I'll remember you for a while
in your imperfect, incomplete life—
a gesture arrested, a speech interrupted,
a thought unspoken, a problem unsolved

With a swift movement of decision,
I pull out my bookmark
and take you back
to the library.

# The Reader's Song

*with a bow to T.S. Eliot*


Can you taste the salt
of Ahab's ocean
O reader, reader?

Did you wait with Tess,
O reader, reader,
leaning on the cold indifferent stones,
waiting for the dawn
that brings her death?

Reader, O reader,
can you hear the wind
calling on the moor,
rattling the casement panes:
Catherine, Catherine!

Are you grateful, reader,
gentle reader, to settle
near a tasseled shaded light,
smooth a fresh-turned page,
and learn the green and ordered
confines of life
at Mansfield Park?

O reader, wait!
Listen to the waves
at Paumanok, listen to the call
of love eternal, grief
and death and death
and birth and birth and birth.

O reader, reader, look:
here's our love song:
may we always know then
you and I
reader, gracious reader,
that no matter who may come and go
our lives are changed forever
by what's written in a book.

# Reader, I Married Him, but…

On our tenth anniversary, I look back over
the years, the quiet years since that rainy
evening when I first saw Ferndean
and saw him again. We have been true
companions ever since, blessed by
marriage in law and spirit. I had dreamed
of this as the best of all lives to live.

Then why—Oh I cannot even think it—
unbidden, with an ache that stops me cold
as I move from room to room in my own
little labors of love—do scenes of holy
loneliness flash upon my inner sight like
lightning, drawing me back as if to the womb?

That plain cottage, where I found my way
back, and my own beloved
Moor House: why do I yearn for them?
They were more time than place. In each,
I owned my life
and lived as I chose.

I draw a breath, shake my head
and almost say aloud,
what nonsense, Jane! You have chosen
this time and place, yes, yearned for this.
Why can you not learn
to be content?

## Timor Mortis: In Praise of the Makars

They were called makars,
poets of dirge and wit
in the cold, perilous courts
of Scottish kings
who understood death
better than life.

The makars sang death and mirth
inside dark squinting stone walls
so all the men and women inside
still bleeding from the barren winds
might know the power of the unknowable,
named and invoked, invincible, merciless,
creator of love, honor, and music.

The makars knew how to see
outside the narrow windows
to trees bearing fruit,
knew how to tease laughter
from disease-ridden stony corners,
knew how to make music of despair.

In fear of death, they made poetry
in the northern darkness
while the dying cried out in their beds
and their greatest king bled to death
in battle beside his thrashing horse.

# Letting Go

Here's a poem
about painting a picture.
While I was writing it,
part of me left

and went back to mixing paint,
wondering if the accident would happen again,
if the colors would work the way they should
and bring light to some part of the world,

if this humble painter would know
when to stop stabbing the brush at the picture
in time to save the suddenness of it all,

and so in the middle of this poem
the words went tap tap tap
in nervous apprehension
and like the painting
breathed rapidly on their own

while the painter and the poet both
stepped back to see
what had happened.

# About the Author

Marydale Stewart is a retired English teacher, administrative librarian, and technical writer and editor and has lived in Illinois, Kansas, and Colorado. She received her Ph.D. at Northern Illinois University and taught at NIU and a number of community colleges.

Her chapbook *Inheritance* was published in 2008 by Puddin'head Press, Chicago. She has two full-length poetry collections, *Let the Thunder In*, published in 2014 by Boxing Day Books, Princeton, IL, and *Risk*, by Kelsay Books, Hemet, CA, in 2017. Her novel *The Wanderers* was published by Black Rose Writing, Castroville, TX, in 2017.

She has poems in *After Hours, Ascent, Assisi, the Aurorean, Boston Literary Magazine, Chocorua Review, DoveTales, Eternal Haunted Summer, Foundling Review, Fredericksburg Literary Review, Friends Journal, Midwestern Gothic, Northwind, River Oak Review, Willow Review,* and *Writers Resist*, and anthologies *A Quiet Shelter There*, Hadley Rille Books, 2015, and *Secrets and Dreams*, Kind of a Hurricane Press, 2016.

www.ingramcontent.com/pod-product-compliance
Lightning Source LLC
LaVergne TN
LVHW021622080426
835510LV00019B/2712